# BLENDER DRINKS

## From Smoothies and Protein Shakes to Adult Beverages

Joanna White

BRISTOL PUBLISHING ENTERPRISES

San Leandro, California

# A nitty gritty® Cookbook

Printed in the United States of America.

ISBN: 1-55867-273-7

Cover design: Frank J. Paredes
Cover photography: John A. Benson
Food stylist: Susan Devaty
Illustrator: Caryn Leschen

# CONTENTS

# INTRODUCTION

Blenders allow you to create almost endless numbers of beverage combinations. Whatever your busy morning routine, you can enjoy a quick, wholesome breakfast with a blended protein drink. In the evening, you can whip together some awesome adult beverages when company drops in unexpectedly. This book ranges from delicious super creamy milkshakes to very sophisticated alcoholic drinks. Included are recipes for smoothies, protein drinks, espresso drinks, frozen or slushy drinks and an assortment of hot and cold drinks including Thai iced tea, creamy carob, spiced chai and fruit-flavored teas.

## BLENDER DO'S AND DON'T'S

1. Follow the manufacturer's instructions regarding capacity of blender and whether or not you can crush ice cubes with your particular model.
2. Fill the blender container only half full when blending thick mixtures.
3. It is best to add liquids first, because it will help feed the solid food into the blades.
4. Add solid foods piece by piece while the motor is running.

5. Be careful not to over-blend when chopping solid foods: pulse on and off until you reach the desired texture.

6. For a coarse chop, blend on low for just a few seconds.

7. During the blending process, occasionally stop the motor and use a spatula to push food from sides of the blender back towards the blades.

8. Never start the motor until the cover is tightly fitted.

9. Do not use a blender to beat egg whites or whipped cream, because the speed will break down the foam while it tries to form.

10. Do not try to mash freshly boiled potatoes in a blender container: they have a tendency to become "gluey" in texture.

11. Because some blenders are not meant to crush ice cubes, I have used crushed ice where ice is required in the recipes. Usually a few ice cubes can be added one at a time to at least 2 cups of liquid while the blender is running, if you desire to cool or thin the beverage.

12. A good rule of thumb is to use twice as much liquid as solids to achieve drinking consistency.

13. To prevent losing carbonation, add carbonated beverages at the end of preparation and blend for just a few seconds before serving.

14. Cut fruits and vegetables into ½- to 1-inch pieces before pureeing.

15. Process dry ingredients, such as candy bars etc., in small batches.

16. Keep frozen peeled bananas on hand to put into blender drinks to add flavor, and to thicken your drink.

17. Because of the chance of salmonella poisoning, DO NOT USE RAW EGGS in your blender drinks.

## SUBSTITUTIONS

When a recipe calls for **cream,** you can substitute half-and-half, coconut cream, whole milk, buttermilk, yogurt, ice cream or frozen yogurt.

For **fresh lemon juice,** use frozen lemon juice or lime juice. I prefer not to use reconstituted lemon juice.

Where **milk** is called for, you can use low-fat milk, rice milk, nut milk, soy milk or carbonated beverages.

For **sugar,** you can also use honey, jam, brown rice syrup, maple syrup, barley malt syrup or stevia.

Note: Stevia is a natural alternative to sugar and is available in health food stores.

## SOME ESSENTIALS TO KEEP ON HAND

- fruit: fresh, frozen or canned
- milk or milk substitutes, half-and-half and/or cream
- fruit juices
- ice cream, frozen yogurt, sherbets, plain or flavored yogurts
- ice cream toppings
- frozen bananas (peeled bananas frozen whole in freezer bags)
- crushed ice
- liqueurs and alcohols for adult beverages, optional
- carbonated beverages: especially lemon-lime, ginger ale and light-flavored sodas
- protein powder or nut butters

## DRINK GARNISHES

*For Sweet Drinks*

- colorful ice cubes: Place a strawberry, wedge of lemon or lime, a strip of citrus peel, berries, mint leaf, etc., in each compartment of an ice-cube tray, fill with water and freeze.

- fruit kebabs: Thread fruit balls such as watermelon, cantaloupe, honeydew, or pieces of fruit such as oranges and limes, or whole fruit like strawberries on a wooden skewer or stir stick.
- citrus wheels: Notch citrus slices (such as oranges, lemons and limes) onto wood skewers with maraschino cherries on either side of the wedge and lay across top of glass.
- candy cane sticks: Use as stirrers or  with marshmallows threaded on.
- whipped cream: Use plain, flavored with extracts and sweetened with sugar, or sweetened with cocoa added.
- mint leaves: Decorate drinks with small clusters of leaves.
- citrus slices or wedges: Lemon, lime, or orange slices make classic garnishes.
- melons: Slice wedges thinly or cut into balls.
- fresh berries: Try raspberries, cranberries, blackberries, blueberries, or cherries.
- cinnamon sticks: Use them as stirrers.
- candied fruit: Decorate drinks with red or green maraschino cherries; or with red, green or yellow pineapple chunks.

- shredded coconut: Use fresh grated or packaged, plain or toasted.
- chocolate: Use white, milk, semi-sweet or dark chocolate, grated or cut into curls.
- spices: Try nutmeg, cinnamon, allspice, cardamom, etc., either sprinkled on top of drink or on top of whipped cream.
- clusters of fruit: Set grapes or other cluster fruit on the edge of the glass.
- shells of fruit: Hollow out a pineapple, coconut shell or melon half and use as a container for drinks.
- flowers: Float edible ("clean") flowers such as orchids and nasturtiums on drinks.
- mini-marshmallows: Spear them on cocktail sticks.

*For Vegetable Drinks*
- clusters of greens: parsley or watercress
- vegetables: celery sticks, cucumber sticks, carrot sticks, carrot curls, cherry tomatoes, cocktail onions, slivers of scallions
- chopped herbs: scallions, chives, parsley or cilantro
- spices: black pepper, paprika or spices used in drinks
- black or green olives

# SMOOTHIES

8    Creamy Pumpkin Smoothie
9    Peachy Cream
10   Orange Papaya Cream
11   Strawberry Pineapple Smoothie
12   Apricot Citrus Refresher
13   Zesty Tomato Smoothie
14   Melon Cucumber Cooler
15   Strawberry Melon Chill
16   Nectarine and Plum Smoothie
17   Prune Orange Smoothie
18   Mixed Fruit Smoothie
19   Honeydew Smoothie
20   Orange Cranberry Smoothie
21   Watermelon Grape Smoothie
22   Pineapple Coconut Smoothie
23   Grape Cranberry Smoothie
24   Orange Blitz
25   Fresh Grape Cooler

# CREAMY PUMPKIN SMOOTHIE

*If you chill the pumpkin and evaporated milk, your drink will have a nice thick consistency.*

1 1/2 cups milk, rice milk or soy milk
1 cup crushed ice
1 can (15 oz.) pure solid pumpkin
1 cup vanilla yogurt or vanilla frozen yogurt
1/3 cup honey, or 1/2 cup sugar
1/4 tsp. pumpkin pie spice
sweetened whipped cream and nutmeg or cinnamon for garnish, optional

Place milk and crushed ice in a blender container and process until smooth. Add remaining ingredients and process on high until smooth. Taste and add more honey or pumpkin pie spice. Garnish with a dollop of whipped cream and a sprinkling of cinnamon or nutmeg if desired.

# PEACHY CREAM

Makes 5 cups

*This creamy concoction is a hit with everyone. Nectarines or mangoes can be substituted for peaches. If you wish, garnish with whipped cream.*

1 cup sliced peaches, fresh or canned
1 medium banana, sliced
1 cup crushed ice
2 cups milk, rice milk or soy milk
1 cup plain yogurt
1–2 tbs. sugar or honey, or more to taste
1/2 tsp. vanilla extract
1 pinch salt

If using fresh peaches, peel and seed. Add all ingredients to a blender container and process on high for at least 1 minute, or until smooth. Taste and add more sweetener if desired.

SMOOTHIES    9

# ORANGE PAPAYA CREAM

*For a nice variation on this smoothie, try mangoes instead of papayas. Lime sherbet can be substituted for orange sherbet.*

1 large fresh papaya
2 cups milk, half-and-half or cream
2 cups orange sherbet

Peel and remove seeds from papaya. Scoop flesh into a blender container, add milk and sherbet and process until smooth. Serve immediately.

# STRABERRY PINEAPPLE SMOOTHIE

Makes 4 cups

*This delicious drink is refreshing and satisfying. Raspberries or Marionberries can be substituted for strawberries, but be sure to sieve the mixture before serving.*

1 cup pineapple juice
3/4 cup sliced strawberries
3/4 cup crushed ice
1/2 cup orange juice
1/2 medium banana, or more to taste
2 tbs. coconut cream
honey to taste, optional

Place pineapple juice, strawberries, ice, orange juice, banana and coconut in a blender container and process on high for at least 1 minute, or until smooth. If using frozen berries, consider adding more banana or a little honey to sweeten.

# APRICOT CITRUS REFRESHER

*Serve this drink in a tall glass with lots of ice. Peaches may be substituted for the apricots. Add plain yogurt or lemon sherbet if you wish to have a creamier drink.*

1 cup canned apricots, with juice
1/3 cup lime juice
1 tbs. lemon juice
1 cup orange juice
1 1/2 cups lime soda
1 pinch salt

Place all ingredients in a blender container and process on high until smooth.

# ZESTY TOMATO SMOOTHIE

*Tomatoes mixed with citric acid in lime and lemon juice give this drink a hot and spicy flavor. If you desire a real kick to your drink, add a few dashes of Tabasco Sauce.*

1 can (14½ oz.) stewed tomatoes, with juice
2 tbs. lime juice
2 tbs. lemon juice
1 cup cold water
½ cup crushed ice
1 tsp. sugar, or more to taste

Place tomatoes in a blender container and process until tomatoes are pureed. Add remaining ingredients and blend until smooth. Taste and add more sugar if desired.

# MELON CUCUMBER COOLER

*This surprising combination really works. Use only fresh mint in this drink. A good garnish would be a thin slice of watermelon and some mint leaves. I prefer to use English cucumber if it is available.*

2 cups seedless watermelon cubes, cut into $1/2$-inch cubes
1 cup honeydew or cantaloupe cubes, cut into $1/2$-inch cubes
$1/2$ cucumber, peeled, seeded and cubed
$1/2$ cup cold water
$1/2$ cup crushed ice
2 tbs. sugar, or more to taste
2 tbs. chopped mint leaves, or more to taste

Make sure melon and cucumber are well chilled. Place watermelon, honeydew, cucumber, water and ice in a blender container and process until smooth. Cut sugar and mint leaves together until finely chopped. Add to melon mixture and process to mix. Taste and add more sweeteners if desired.

# STRAWBERRY MELON CHILL

*Black pepper may seem an odd ingredient but it really enhances the strawberry flavor of this drink. It is important that you use just a very small amount of pepper.*

2 cups strawberries
1 cup finely diced seedless watermelon
1 cup chilled orange juice
¾ cup crushed ice
2 tbs. lime juice
1 tbs. honey, or more to taste
1 small pinch black pepper

Place all ingredients in a blender container and process on high until smooth. Taste and add more honey if desired.

strawberry

# NECTARINE AND PLUM SMOOTHIE

*The advantage of using nectarines and plums is that these fruits do not have to be peeled. Peaches could be substituted for nectarines, but they must be peeled first. You may need to increase the amount of sweetener, depending on the ripeness of the fruit.*

2 nectarines
2 plums
1 cup vanilla yogurt
1 cup cold milk, rice milk or soy milk
½ cup crushed ice
1 pinch nutmeg
1–2 tbs. honey or sugar, or to taste, optional

Seed nectarines and plums and chop coarsely. Add to a blender container along with remaining ingredients. Blend until smooth, taste and add more sweetener if desired.

# PRUNE ORANGE SMOOTHIE

*This is a great breakfast smoothie that can be enhanced with protein powder if desired. For an alternative, substitute orange sherbet for vanilla ice cream.*

1 cup cooked pitted prunes
2/3 cup orange juice, or more to taste
1 1/2 cups milk, or more to taste
1 1/2 cups vanilla ice cream or frozen yogurt
2 tsp. fresh lemon juice
2 tbs. sugar or honey

Process prunes until mushy. Add remaining ingredients and process until smooth and creamy. Add more milk or orange juice to thin, if desired.

# MIXED FRUIT SMOOTHIE

*This is a delicious way to start the day. Depending on the ripeness of the fruit, you may want to add a little brown sugar for additional sweetness.*

½ cup sliced fresh strawberries
½ cup cantaloupe
½ cup diced fresh papaya or mango
½ cup honey
½ cup orange juice or papaya juice
1 cup plain or vanilla yogurt
1 cup crushed ice
extra fruit pieces for garnish

Place all ingredients in a blender container and process until smooth. Garnish with a piece of one of the fruits used in recipe.

# HONEYDEW SMOOTHIE

*For the best flavor, choose very ripe honeydew melons. This recipe is very refreshing and can be altered by using lemon juice in place of lime juice. If desired, add a little fresh ginger for a slight touch of heat.*

2 cups diced honeydew melon
6 tbs. lime juice
2 tbs. chopped fresh mint leaves
1/2–1 cup water or lemon-lime soda
1 cup chopped ice
honey or sugar to taste, optional

Place all ingredients except honey in a blender container and process until smooth. If using soda instead of water, add soda at the last minute. Taste and add sweetener if desired.

# ORANGE CRANBERRY SMOOTHIE

Makes: 5-6 cups

*Oranges and cranberries marry well. Fresh oranges can be substituted for canned Mandarin oranges, but I would advise sieving the mixture. Garnish with orange slices.*

1 cup Mandarin oranges, drained
2 cups cranberry juice
1 cup orange sherbet
1 cup crushed ice
1 cup orange soda
$1/2$–1 cup vanilla ice cream

Place oranges, juice, sherbet and ice in a blender container and process until smooth. Add orange soda and blend to mix. Taste and add ice cream if desired.

# WATERMELON GRAPE SMOOTHIE

*This is a refreshing drink which is enhanced by chilling the watermelon and soda before blending. Citrus-flavored soda can be substituted for grape soda. Garnish with a slice of watermelon and/or a small cluster of grapes.*

3 cups diced seedless watermelon
1 cup crushed ice
1 1/2 cups grape soda
1–2 tsp. sugar or honey, or to taste, optional

Blend watermelon and ice on high until smooth. Add soda, quickly blend, taste and add sweetener if desired.

# PINEAPPLE COCONUT SMOOTHIE

Makes: 4½ cups

*Most major grocery stores now carry a wonderful assortment of juices. Pineapple-coconut juice is one of my favorites because it naturally has a creamy texture. Garnish with a slice of lime or pineapple.*

2 cups purchased pineapple-coconut juice
1½ cups diced mixed peeled fruit (cantaloupe, honeydew, peaches, watermelon or other)
1 cup lime sherbet
1 cup crushed ice

Place all ingredients in a blender container and process on high until smooth.

# GRAPE CRANBERRY SMOOTHIE

*The sweetness of the grapes and mixed fruit will determine if you need to add honey or sugar in this recipe. Ice cream, frozen yogurt or raspberry sherbet can be substituted for cream and the amount is determined by your personal taste. Garnish with a small cluster of grapes or a piece of fruit.*

1 cup seedless green or red grapes
1 1/2 cups cranberry juice
1 cup diced mixed fruit, peeled (peach, pear, melon, mango, papaya or other)
1 cup crushed ice
2–4 tbs. cream, or to taste
1–2 tbs. honey or sugar, or to taste, optional

Place all ingredients except sweetener in a blender container and process on high until smooth. Taste and add sweetener if desired. Sieve mixture before serving.

# ORANGE BLITZ

*In this drink, the flavor is enhanced by using frozen orange soda instead of water or ice cubes. A good trick when making punch is to make an ice ring using one of the juices in the punch recipe, so that when the ice melts it does not dilute the drink. To make the ice ring, pour liquid of choice into a gelatin mold or tube cake pan and freeze.*

1 cup orange soda
1 cup orange juice
1 cup canned Mandarin orange slices, drained
1 cup orange sherbet or sorbet

Pour orange soda into ice cube trays and freeze solid. When frozen, crush into smaller pieces. Place all ingredients in a blender container and process until smooth. Serve immediately.

# FRESH GRAPE COOLER

Makes: 5 cups

*This recipe has a great flavor and can be made into a breakfast drink by adding 1 or 2 tbs. protein powder and substituting vanilla yogurt for ice cream. Garnish with a small cluster of grapes.*

3 cups seedless green grapes
2 cups citrus or lemon-lime soda
1 cup vanilla ice cream
1 cup crushed ice
1–2 tbs. sugar or honey, optional

Place all ingredients in a blender container and process on high until smooth. Taste and add sweetener if desired. Sieve if you desire a smooth drink.

# PROTEIN AND HEALTHY SHAKES

# TROPICAL BLITZ

*Passion fruit juice is often available in the frozen juice section of major grocery stores. Mango, if out of season, is available canned. If you choose to use coconut flakes, you can get a nuttier flavor by toasting flakes under a broiler until brown before blending.*

$1/2$ cup mango chunks, fresh or canned
1 cup crushed ice
$1/3$ cup orange juice
$1/3$ cup passion fruit juice
$1/3$ cup guava juice
3 tbs. coconut cream or coconut flakes
2 tbs. wheat germ
1–2 tbs. protein powder, optional
1 large scoop vanilla frozen yogurt, or fruit flavor of choice
1 medium banana, cut into chunks

Place all ingredients in a blender container and process on high for several minutes until well mixed.

# POTASSIUM POWER

*This makes a wonderful high-energy drink that is loaded with potassium. Plain vanilla yogurt can be substituted for frozen yogurt. Add 1 to 2 tbs. carob powder or chocolate sauce for a chocolate-banana flavor.*

1½ frozen bananas
2 cups frozen vanilla or banana yogurt
¾ cup milk, rice milk, almond milk or soy milk
1 tbs. brewer's yeast
1½ tbs. wheat germ
1½ tbs. lecithin powder or granules
1–2 tbs. honey, molasses or sugar, to taste

Cut bananas into 1-inch chunks, place in a blender container and process for 15 seconds. Add remaining ingredients and blend for 1 minute or until smooth. Taste and add more sweetener if desired.

# STRAWBERRY CRÈME

*Always use fresh strawberries when available. Use the least amount of sweetener until you have tasted. I like to use strawberry frozen yogurt or strawberry-flavored yogurt for extra flavor.*

1 cup sliced strawberries, fresh or frozen
1½ cups frozen yogurt or regular yogurt, strawberry or vanilla preferred
½ cup milk, almond milk, rice milk or soy milk
2 tbs. protein powder
2 tbs. strawberry jam, honey, barley rice syrup or sugar, or to taste

Blend strawberries for 15 seconds. Add remaining ingredients and process until smooth. Taste and adjust sweetness.

# APRICOT-ALMOND ALTERNATIVE

*Almond or other nut butters make a good alternative to protein powder for blender drinks. Nut butter adds flavor and creates a slightly denser texture in your shakes.*

2 cups mashed apricots, fresh or canned
1 cup almond milk, soy milk, rice milk or milk
1 cup plain or vanilla yogurt
$1/2$ cup crushed ice
$1/2$ cup almond butter
1–2 tbs. apricot jam or honey, optional
few drops almond extract, optional

Place all ingredients except jam and almond extract in a blender container and process until smooth. Taste and add jam or almond extract for more flavor if desired.

# ISLAND CHILL

*Guava juice is available bottled or frozen. Make sure juices are chilled before blending. Serve in a large glass with a wedge of fresh pineapple for garnish.*

1 cup guava juice
1 cup cherry or berry juice
1 cup pineapple juice
1 cup water or soda
1 cup crushed ice
2 tbs. protein powder
2 tbs. coconut cream
sugar or honey to taste, optional

Place all ingredients except sugar in a blender container and process on high until smooth. Taste and add a little sugar or honey to taste if desired.

# HAWAIIAN FLING

Makes 4½ cups

*Guava or papaya juice can be substituted for pineapple or orange juice in this recipe. Always chill juices before using. It is nice to serve this with a skewer of fresh fruit such as pineapple chunks, orange wedges or maraschino cherries.*

1 cup pineapple juice
1 cup orange juice
3 tbs. grenadine syrup
¼ cup lime juice
2 tbs. fresh lemon juice
2 tbs. protein powder (prefer fruit-flavored)
½ cup plain yogurt or fruit sherbet, or more to taste
1½ cups crushed ice

In a blender container, combine all ingredients and process on high until mixture is smooth and creamy.

# CREAMY MANDARIN ORANGE

Makes 4 cups

*This recipe makes a delicious breakfast drink with a wonderful intense flavor. Garnish with a slice of orange on the edge of the glass.*

1 can (15 oz.) Mandarin oranges, drained
1 cup orange yogurt or orange sherbet
$1/2$ cup sweetened condensed milk
1 cup crushed ice
$1/4$ cup fresh lemon or lime juice
1 tbs. protein powder, or more if desired
$1/2$ cup milk or orange juice to thin, optional

Place all ingredients in a blender container and process on high for several minutes to fully incorporate oranges. Taste and thin mixture with milk or orange juice if desired.

# DATE-ALMOND SHAKE

*This recipe uses almond milk, which is high in protein and calcium. If you wish more protein, simply add protein powder to this recipe.*

2 cups fresh *Almond Milk*, page 35
3 frozen bananas
12 pitted dates
1/2 cup crushed ice
few drops banana or almond extract,
   optional

Place all ingredients in a blender container and process on high until smooth. Taste and add banana or almond extract for more taste if desired.

# ALMOND MILK

*This simple nut milk is best when made fresh. Always use blanched almonds (without skins) for white-colored nut milk.*

2 cups cold water
$1/2$ cup blanched almonds
$1\,1/2$ tbs. pure maple syrup

Place cold water and almonds in a blender container and process on high for several minutes, until mixture turns white. Pour into a fine sieve. Add maple syrup to taste. Refrigerate until ready to serve.

# CAROB YOGURT CREAM

Makes 3½ cups

*Carob is a healthy alternative to chocolate. If you like to use soy products, use soy milk, soy protein or tofu in place of protein powder. Chocolate syrup can be substituted for carob if desired.*

3 cups low-fat frozen vanilla or chocolate yogurt
¼ cup soy milk, almond milk or rice milk
¼ cup carob syrup or powder, or more to taste
2–3 tbs. honey or brown rice syrup, or more to taste
2 tbs. protein powder

Place all ingredients in a blender container and process until smooth. Taste and add more sweetener or carob syrup if desired.

# PINEAPPLE-ALMOND DRINK

Makes 2½ cups

*This is an easy breakfast drink that uses almond butter in place of powdered protein. Cashew butter can be substituted for almond butter.*

1 frozen banana
1 cup chilled pineapple juice
½ cup papaya juice
¼ cup almond butter
1–2 tbs. honey or brown rice syrup, optional

Cut frozen banana into 1-inch cubes. Place banana, juices and almond butter in a blender container and process on high until mixture is smooth. Taste and add honey for sweetness if desired.

# APRICOT EGGNOG SHAKE

*This shake has a wonderful golden color and tastes great. If eggnog ice cream is not available use French vanilla ice cream and substitute eggnog for milk.*

¾ cup apricot puree
1 cup eggnog ice cream
¾ tsp. fresh lemon juice
½ cup milk, or more to thin
1 tbs. protein powder
1 pinch mace

Place all ingredients in a blender container and process until smooth. Serve immediately.

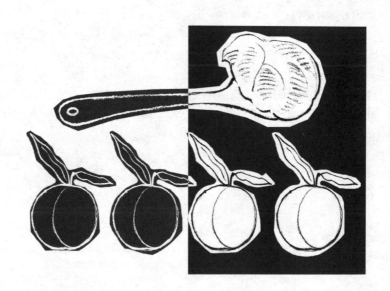

# PRUNE APPLE CREAM

*The protein in this drink comes in the form of almond butter and yogurt. If you wish more protein, add 1 to 2 tbs. protein powder. If you wish to make a thicker drink, add about ½ cup crushed ice.*

1 cup chilled unsweetened prune juice
1 cup chilled unsweetened apple juice (prefer unfiltered)
1 tbs. almond butter
½ cup plain or vanilla yogurt or frozen yogurt
1 tsp. toasted sesame oil
1 tbs. honey, or to taste, optional

Place all ingredients except honey in a blender container and process until smooth. Taste and add honey to sweeten if desired.

# MANGO MORNING DRINK

*This recipe is very satisfying and flavorful. If you choose, you can use buttermilk in place of yogurt. Also, papaya juice can be substituted for orange juice.*

1½ cups diced mangoes
1 cup orange juice
1½ cups plain, vanilla or orange yogurt
1–2 tbs. protein powder
¾ cup crushed ice
1–2 tsp. lemon or lime juice
honey or sugar to taste, optional

Place mangoes in a blender container and process for 30 seconds. Add juice, yogurt, protein powder, ice and lemon juice and process until smooth. Taste and add honey or sugar to sweeten if desired.

# CARROT TOMATO PICK-ME-UP

Makes: 2½ cups

*I like to make this drink when I need a quick pick-me-up. This recipe can be served at room temperature or the tomato juice and broth can be heated and then blended. Carrots actually blend well when mixed with enough liquid. It is important to follow the technique described below.*

2 medium carrots, peeled and coarsely chopped
1 cup tomato juice
1 cup chicken or vegetable broth
2 tbs. sour cream, or more to taste
1 dash white pepper
1 dash Worcestershire sauce or Tabasco Sauce

Place carrots in a blender container and chop until finely minced. Add tomato juice and process on medium-high until mixture is pureed. Add remaining ingredients and process on high until mixture is smooth. Taste and add more sour cream or flavorings if desired. If you like a smoother consistency, sieve mixture before serving.

# CITRUS BLEND

*This delightful blend is a refreshing way to start the day. A slice of orange and a pineapple wedge would be an ideal garnish.*

1 cup orange juice
1 cup orange sherbet
½ cup pineapple coconut juice
1 tsp. lime juice, or more to taste
1 cup crushed ice
1 cup lemon-lime soda

Place all ingredients except soda in a blender container and process on high until smooth. Add soda and barely blend. Taste and add more lime juice if desired.

# FRUITED RICE MILK

Makes: 4½ cups

*Rice milk is a great alternative to cow's milk and is now available in most major grocery stores. This drink ("horchata") is very popular in Mexico and is generally served over ice. This recipe includes fruit, but it is also commonly served without fruit.*

3 cups chilled rice milk
1½ cups chopped fruit: strawberries, mangoes, papayas or other
¾ tsp. vanilla extract
¼ tsp. cinnamon
1–2 tbs. sweetened condensed milk, or to taste, optional

Place all ingredients except condensed milk in a blender container and process until smooth. Taste and add condensed milk for a sweeter, creamier flavor if desired. Serve in a tall glass filled with ice cubes.

# ADULT BEVERAGES

45  Strawberry-Banana Daiquiri
46  Peach Margarita
47  Margarita Special
48  Lemon Chill
49  Peach Bellini
50  Pink Lemonade
51  Chocolate Gorilla
52  Strawberry Creamsicle
53  Killer Kahlua
54  Chocolate Amaretto Cream

55  Raspberry Kiss
56  Creamy Fuzzy Peach
57  Tropical Martini
58  Mandarin Madness
59  Melon Chill
60  Almond Joy
61  Rainbowcicle
62  Watermelon Cream
63  Fruited Wine Chill
64  Wine Cooler

# STRAWBERRY-BANANA DAIQUIRI

*A standard daiquiri is made with lime, rum, crushed ice and maybe a little sugar. This recipe takes it to a more memorable and sweeter level. Serve in a large saucer champagne glass.*

1 cup fresh or frozen strawberries
$1/2$ fresh or frozen banana
1 tbs. fresh lime juice
2 oz. gold rum
1 oz. dark rum
1 cup crushed ice
1–3 tsp. sugar, optional

Place all ingredients in a blender container and process on high until mixture is slushy. If using frozen strawberries, add sugar to taste.

# PEACH MARGARITA

*This is a perfect drink to serve with a Mexican meal. If you choose to use fresh peaches, you may need to add a little sugar if the peaches are not perfectly ripe.*

1 cup canned or fresh peaches
1 can (6 oz.) frozen lemonade concentrate
3 oz. tequila, or more to taste
1 cup crushed ice

Place all ingredients in a blender container and process until mixture is slushy. Pour into a large glass rimmed with lemon juice and kosher salt.

# MARGARITA SPECIAL

*This potent drink can set you on fire! Rim the glass with lemon juice and kosher salt. Serve with a slice of fresh lime.*

2 oz. gold tequila
1 oz. Triple Sec
2 tbs. lime juice
2 cups crushed ice
Grand Marnier to float

Place tequila, Triple Sec, lime juice and ice in a blender container and process until mixture is slushy. Serve in a kosher salt-rimmed glass and pour just enough Grand Marnier to float on top.

# LEMON CHILL

*This zesty drink would be a good precursor to heavy appetizers or a large meat meal. Serve in a glass rimmed with lemon juice and dipped in fine sugar.*

2 oz. vodka or citron vodka
1 oz. Triple Sec
12 oz. lemonade (not the pink variety)
2 tsp. lemon zest
2 cups crushed ice

Place all ingredients in a blender container and process until slushy. Serve in sugar-rimmed glasses with a twist of lemon peel.

# PEACH BELLINI

*This sweet drink can be made creamy with the addition of ice cream if desired. A slice of peach with a sprig of mint on the side of the glass can be used as a garnish.*

1 cup canned or fresh peaches, chilled
6 oz. champagne
1–2 oz. peach liqueur
1½ cups crushed ice
1 cup vanilla or peach ice cream, optional

Place all ingredients in a blender container and process until smooth. Taste and add ice cream if desired. Serve with or without ice cubes.

# PINK LEMONADE

*Citron vodka has a distinct lemon flavor that goes perfectly with lemonade-based drinks. Chambord is a delicious raspberry liqueur that makes a good balance to the tartness of lemon.*

1 1/2 cups lemonade
3 oz. citron vodka
2 oz. Chambord liqueur
1 1/2 cups crushed ice

Place all the ingredients in a blender container and process until slushy. Serve with a slice of lemon or a twist of lemon peel.

# CHOCOLATE GORILLA

*This is reminiscent of a chocolate banana shake. You can intensify the chocolate flavor by using chocolate ice cream but this will dilute the banana flavor somewhat. Garnish with a dollop of whipped cream and a drizzle of chocolate syrup or a chocolate swizzle stick.*

2 tbs. chocolate syrup
1 frozen banana
1 cup vanilla or banana ice cream
2 oz. crème de cacao liqueur
1 oz. banana liqueur
sweetened whipped cream or *Chocolate Whipped Cream*, page 109, for garnish

Place syrup, banana, ice cream, crème de cacao and banana liqueur in a blender container and process until smooth. Garnish with sweetened whipped cream or *Chocolate Whipped Cream.*

# STRAWBERRY CREAMSICLE

*If you desire a less fattening version of this recipe, use low-fat frozen yogurt instead of ice cream. Garnish with a fresh strawberry and mint leaves. Frozen strawberries can be used in place of fresh strawberries.*

1 cup sliced fresh strawberries
1 cup strawberry or vanilla ice cream
2 oz. vodka
1 oz. amaretto liqueur
ice cubes

Place strawberries, ice cream, vodka and liqueur in a blender container and process until smooth. Serve in a glass with a few ice cubes.

# KILLER KAHLUA

*Kahlua is a very popular coffee-flavored liqueur. A dollop of sweetened whipped cream topped with a chocolate covered coffee bean makes a trendy garnish for this drink.*

2 oz. Kahlua liqueur
1 oz. crème de cacao liqueur
1 ½ cups vanilla or coffee ice cream
ice cubes
sweetened whipped cream for garnish

Place liqueurs and ice cream in a blender container and process until smooth. Serve over ice and garnish with sweetened whipped cream.

# CHOCOLATE AMARETTO CREAM

Servings: 2

*Amaretto is an almond-flavored liqueur that really goes well with chocolate. This drink is good served over ice, or garnished with a dollop of whipped cream or a small scoop of ice cream. Tuaca liqueur is flavored with citrus and vanilla.*

1 oz. amaretto liqueur
2 tbs. chocolate syrup
1 oz. Tuaca Italian liqueur
1 ½ cups vanilla ice cream
ice cubes

Place amaretto, syrup, Tuaca and ice cream in a blender container and process until smooth. Serve over ice cubes.

54    ADULT BEVERAGES

# RASPBERRY KISS

*Two berry liqueurs, champagne and raspberries makes an intense fruit-flavored drink that is enhanced even further by raspberry sherbet. Sometimes raspberry ice cream or frozen yogurt is available which really makes a creamy, full-flavored drink.*

1 cup fresh or frozen raspberries
1 oz. Chambord liqueur
1 oz. crème de cassis liqueur
1 cup champagne
1 cup raspberry sherbet or vanilla ice cream
ice cubes

Place raspberries, liqueurs, champagne and sherbet in a blender container and process until smooth. Sieve to remove seeds and serve over ice cubes.

# CREAMY FUZZY PEACH

Servings: 2

*Frozen yogurt can be substituted for ice cream for a lighter drink. If using canned peaches, be sure to drain off the syrup.*

2 oz. amaretto liqueur
2 oz. peach schnapps
1 cup canned peaches, drained, or
   fresh peaches
1 1/2 cups orange sherbet or vanilla ice
   cream
ice cubes

Place liquors, peaches and ice cream in a blender container and process until smooth. Serve over ice cubes.

# TROPICAL MARTINI

*I think this drink is a great improvement on a dry martini. If you wish a garnish, serve with a long wedge of fresh pineapple.*

3 oz. citron vodka
1/2 cup chilled passion fruit juice
1/2 cup chopped mangoes
1/2 cup chilled, unsweetened
   pineapple juice
1 cup crushed ice

Place all ingredients in a blender container and process until mixture is slushy.

# MANDARIN MADNESS

*Mandarin vodka is perfect for this citrus concoction. This refreshing drink is ideal to serve on a hot day or as a precursor to a heavy meal.*

1 cup orange juice
$1/4$ cup lemon juice
2 tbs. lime juice
2 oz. Absolut Mandarin vodka
2 tsp. sugar
2 cups crushed ice
orange, lemon and lime slices for garnish

Place all ingredients in a blender container and process until slushy. Use slices of all three citrus fruits as garnish on the rim of a large glass.

# MELON CHILL

Servings: 2

*This delicious simple drink makes a hit at picnics. Honeydew melon can be substituted for watermelon. Make sure melon is well chilled before using.*

1 cup diced watermelon
1/2 cup lemonade
2 oz. Midori liqueur or melon liqueur
1/2 cup crushed ice

Place all ingredients in a blender container and process until slushy. Serve with a thick wedge of watermelon or a lemon slice.

# ALMOND JOY

*This is a favorite mix that always gets rave reviews. Serve in a tall glass with lots of ice cubes.*

1 oz. crème de cacao liqueur
1 oz. amaretto liqueur
1 oz. Kahlua liqueur
2 cups cream or half-and-half

Blend all ingredients together until well combined and serve over ice.

# RAINBOWCICLE

*Rainbow sherbet is generally made with orange, lime and raspberry flavors. Another version uses pineapple with orange and lime. If using the pineapple variety, it is best to sieve the mixture before serving. Garnish with slices of orange, lemon and lime for a rainbow effect.*

1 cup orange juice
1 cup rainbow sherbet
2 oz. vodka
1–2 oz. orange curaçao
1 cup crushed ice

Place all ingredients in a blender container and process on high until smooth. Serve immediately.

# WATERMELON CREAM

*Sherbet makes a lighter drink but vanilla or raspberry ice cream also works well in this recipe. Garnish with a slice of watermelon or a few fresh raspberries. If you wish a stronger drink, add 1 ounce Midori liqueur as a floater.*

2½ cups diced, seedless watermelon
1 cup rainbow or raspberry sherbet or vanilla ice cream, or more to taste
3 oz. vodka
1 cup crushed ice

   Place all ingredients in a blender container and process on high until smooth. Add more sherbet or vanilla ice cream for a creamier drink.

# FRUITED WINE CHILL

Makes: 4½ cups

*The amount of wine in this drink is up to your personal taste, so adjust the amount of soda as desired. Garnish with a cinnamon stick or piece of fruit used in the recipe.*

1 cup sweet wine (prefer Muscat blanc, Malvasia Bianca or Muscat Canelli)
1½ cups diced, peeled non citrus fruit: peach, melon, plum, papaya, grapes or other
1 tsp. lemon juice
1 dash cinnamon
1 dash ground cloves
1 cup crushed ice
1 cup lemon-lime soda
1–2 tsp. sugar or honey, or to taste, optional

Place wine, fruit, lemon juice, spices and ice in a blender container and process until smooth. Blend in soda, taste and add sweetener if desired.

# WINE COOLER

*Choose your favorite sweet wine and sparkle it up with lemonade and lemon soda. Garnish with a slice of lemon and/or a small cluster of grapes.*

1 cup sweet red or white wine
1 cup lemonade
1 cup crushed ice
¼ cup grenadine syrup, or to taste
1 cup lemon or lemon-lime soda

Place all ingredients except soda in a blender container and process on high until smooth. Quickly blend in soda, taste and increase grenadine syrup for additional sweetness if desired.

# ESPRESSO DRINKS

66    White Chocolate Raspberry Latte
67    Caramel Royale
68    Iced Frappuccino
69    Vanilla Honey Latte
70    Peanut Butter Espresso
71    Buttery Finger Blitz
72    Ginger Cream
73    Healthy Grain Coffee Latte
74    Chocolate Orange Latte
75    Iced Praline Espresso
76    Chocolate Kahlua Cream
77    Fresh Strawberry Espresso
78    Strawberry Whipped Cream
79    Hazelnut Fudge Latte
80    Iced Cherry Espresso
81    Chocolate Almond Breve
82    Maple Coffee Cream
83    Raspberry Coffee Chill

# WHITE CHOCOLATE RASPBERRY LATTE

Servings: 1

*White chocolate complements raspberry wonderfully. For a little flair, drizzle whipped cream with a little raspberry-flavored syrup for color.*

1 oz. white chocolate
1–2 shots espresso, to taste
2 tbs. raspberry-flavored syrup
6–8 oz. steamed milk, to taste
sweetened whipped cream for garnish

In a blender container, chop white chocolate into small pieces. Add hot espresso shots and raspberry syrup. Blend until chocolate melts. Pour into a large mug and gently stir in steamed milk. Garnish with a dollop of whipped cream.

# CARAMEL ROYALE

*It is important to warm the caramel so it mixes well with the coffee and keeps the liquid hot. Consider drizzling a little caramel over the whipped cream for effect.*

1–2 shots espresso, to taste
3 tbs. warm caramel sauce, or more to taste
1 tbs. dark chocolate ice cream topping
1 tbs. vanilla-flavored syrup, or $\frac{1}{2}$ tsp. vanilla
    extract
6–8 oz. steamed milk, to taste
sweetened whipped cream for garnish

In a blender container, combine espresso, warm caramel sauce, topping and syrup. Pour into a cup and gently stir in steamed milk. Top with whipped cream.

# ICED FRAPPUCCINO

*This iced coffee drink is refreshing and mentally energizing. Serve this decadent drink on a hot afternoon.*

1–2 shots espresso, to taste
3 tbs. chocolate syrup
$\frac{1}{2}$ scoop coffee ice cream
6–8 oz. cold milk, to taste
1 scoop coffee ice cream for topping

Blend espresso, chocolate syrup and $\frac{1}{2}$ scoop of coffee ice cream until mixture is smooth. Pour into a tall glass partially filled with ice. Add cold milk and a scoop of coffee ice cream on top.

# VANILLA HONEY LATTE

*Honey can be a very satisfying flavor. Consider drizzling a little honey on top of the whipped cream for garnish.*

1–2 shots espresso, to taste
2–3 tbs. honey, warmed, to taste
1 tbs. vanilla-flavored syrup
6–8 oz. steamed milk, to taste
sweetened whipped cream for garnish

Blend espresso, warm honey and vanilla syrup together until well mixed. Pour into a mug and gently stir in steamed milk. Garnish with a dollop of whipped cream.

# PEANUT BUTTER ESPRESSO

Servings: 1

*This drink is definitely for peanut butter lovers. A fun garnish would be choco-late covered peanuts, peanut M&M's or half a peanut butter cup on top of the whipped cream.*

1–2 shots espresso, to taste
1 tbs. creamy peanut butter
2 tbs. chocolate syrup, or more to taste
6–8 oz. steamed milk, to taste
sweetened whipped cream for garnish

Blend very hot espresso with peanut butter and syrup until smooth. Pour into a mug and stir in steamed milk. Garnish with whipped cream.

# BUTTERY FINGER BLITZ

Servings: 1

*Now there is a Butterfinger ice cream available in grocery stores. A scoop of this would satisfy your sugar cravings for a week. Of course, sweetened whipped cream is another alternative.*

$^1/_2$ Butterfinger peanut bar
1–2 shots espresso, to taste
2 tbs. chocolate syrup
6–8 oz. steamed milk, to taste
1 scoop vanilla ice cream or Butterfinger ice cream for garnish

Cut up Butterfinger and chop in a blender container until crumbly. Reserve 1 tbs. of the crumbs to use as garnish. Add hot espresso and chocolate syrup and blend until smooth. Gently stir in steamed milk and garnish with ice cream. Sprinkle reserved crumbs on top.

# GINGER CREAM

Servings: 1

*Candied ginger is the secret ingredient in this soothing drink. In a pinch, you can substitute ¼ to ½ tsp. powdered ginger and add 1 tbs. sugar.*

4 slices candied ginger
2 shots espresso
8 oz. steamed milk
1 scoop vanilla ice cream

Place ginger in a blender container and chop into small pieces. Pour hot espresso into blender container and process on high for several minutes to thoroughly incorporate ginger. Pour mixture into a mug and gently stir in steamed milk. Serve with a scoop of ice cream on top.

# HEALTHY GRAIN COFFEE LATTE

Servings: 2

*This is for people who love lattes but are trying to get off the caffeine! Carob powder or syrup is the substitute for chocolate. Vanilla soy milk adds wonderful flavor and texture. Regular milk with a few drops of pure vanilla extract can be substituted for vanilla soy milk. Grain coffee is a non-stimulating coffee substitute made from malted barley, chicory and rye.*

2 heaping tsp. grain coffee (prefer Pero brand)
$2/3$ cup vanilla soy milk
2 tsp. carob powder or syrup
2 tsp. brown rice syrup, barley malt syrup or sugar, or more to taste
$1\,1/3$ cups boiling water

Place all ingredients in a blender container and process until smooth and creamy. Serve immediately

# CHOCOLATE ORANGE LATTE

*Chocolate and orange is a popular flavor combination. Orange liqueur can be substituted for orange syrup if you desire something stronger.*

1–2 shots espresso, to taste
1/2 cup chocolate ice cream
2 tbs. orange syrup
6 oz. steamed milk
sweetened whipped cream and chocolate syrup for garnish

In a blender container, process espresso, ice cream and orange syrup together. Gently stir into steamed milk and garnish with whipped cream drizzled with chocolate syrup.

# ICED PRALINE ESPRESSO

Servings: 1

*Praline ice cream is my favorite and is enhanced further by the addition of praline or caramel syrup.*

¹/₂ cup praline ice cream
1–2 tbs. praline or caramel syrup, to taste
2 shots espresso
¹/₂–1 cup cold milk, to taste
ice cubes
whipped cream and caramel syrup for
   garnish

Place ice cream, syrup, espresso and milk in a blender container and process until smooth. Pour into a glass ¹/₂ filled with ice cubes. Garnish with whipped cream and drizzle a little caramel syrup over.

# CHOCOLATE KAHLUA CREAM

Servings: 1

*This is an iced coffee drink that can be enhanced by substituting Kahlua liqueur for Kahlua syrup. Garnish the top with an additional scoop of ice cream or a dollop of whipped cream sprinkled with a little cocoa powder.*

1/2 cup chocolate ice cream
2 tbs. Kahlua syrup or Kahlua liqueur
2 shots espresso
1/2 cup cold milk
ice cubes
whipped cream for garnish

Place ice cream, Kahlua, espresso and milk in a blender container and process until smooth. Serve in a tall glass 3/4 filled with ice cubes and garnish with whipped cream.

# FRESH STRAWBERRY ESPRESSO

*Fresh strawberry puree really makes a delicious iced coffee drink. The trick is to add a tiny sprinkle of pepper to enhance the strawberry flavor. Another alternative for a garnish is* Strawberry Whipped Cream, *page 78.*

½ cup sliced strawberries
1–2 tbs. strawberry syrup, to taste
1 tiny sprinkle black pepper
2 shots espresso
1 cup strawberry ice cream
½ cup cold milk, or more to taste
strawberry ice cream or whipped cream and a fresh strawberry for garnish

Place all ingredients in a blender container and process until smooth. If you like a thinner drink, add a little more milk. Garnish with small scoop of ice cream and a fresh strawberry.

# STRAWBERRY WHIPPED CREAM

*Use this recipe to garnish drinks or as a frosting for cake. Garnish with fresh strawberries.*

1/2 lb. fresh strawberries
sugar to taste
1 tiny sprinkle black pepper
1 cup cream

Place strawberries, sugar and black pepper in a blender container and process into a puree. Using a mixer, whip cream until soft peaks are formed. Gently fold strawberries into whipped cream. Keep refrigerated until ready to serve.

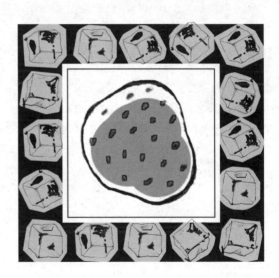

# HAZELNUT FUDGE LATTE

Servings: 1

*This delicious latte should be served with a dollop of sweetened whipped cream and sprinkled with chopped toasted hazelnuts.*

¹/₄ cup hot fudge sauce
1–2 tbs. hazelnut syrup, to taste
2 shots espresso
1 cup steamed milk
whipped cream and chopped nuts for garnish

Place fudge sauce, hazelnut syrup and espresso in a blender container and process until smooth. Gently stir into steamed milk. Garnish with whipped cream and chopped nuts.

# ICED CHERRY ESPRESSO

*This delicious drink can be varied by adding 2 tbs. chocolate syrup or substituting a carbonated soda for milk.*

6 oz. milk
1–2 shots espresso, to taste
1/4 cup chopped maraschino cherries
1 cup cherry or vanilla ice cream
ice cubes
whipped cream and maraschino cherry for garnish

Place milk, espresso, cherries and ice cream in a blender container and process until smooth. Pour into a tall glass partially filled with ice cubes. Garnish with whipped cream and cherry.

# CHOCOLATE ALMOND BREVE

*A breve uses steamed half-and-half in place of steamed milk. Garnish with a sprinkling of toasted chopped almonds or a few chocolate covered almonds on top of whipped cream.*

1–2 shots espresso, to taste
1/2 cup fudge chocolate ice cream
2 tbs. hot thick fudge sauce
2 tbs. almond syrup
6–8 oz. steamed half-and-half, to taste
whipped cream and chopped toasted almonds for garnish

Place espresso, ice cream, fudge sauce and almond syrup in a blender container and process until smooth. Stir into steamed half-and-half. Serve with whipped cream and chopped toasted almonds or chocolate-covered almonds.

# MAPLE COFFEE CREAM

Makes: 4 cups

*If you really like the flavor of maple, try substituting maple ice cream for vanilla ice cream. For a lighter drink, substitute low-fat vanilla frozen yogurt for ice cream.*

2 cups cold coffee
1 ½ cups vanilla ice cream
2 tbs. maple syrup, or to taste
1 cup crushed ice

Place all ingredients in a blender container and process on high until smooth. Taste and add more maple syrup if desired.

# RASPBERRY COFFEE CHILL

Makes: 3¹/₂ cups

*This drink would go well with muffins or toasted multi-grain bread. The chocolate adds a new dimension to the drink. To determine if you like this drink with chocolate syrup added, place a small amount of mixture from the blender in a glass and stir in a few drops of chocolate syrup.*

2 cups cold coffee
1 cup raspberry sherbet
1 cup crushed ice
1–2 tbs. raspberry jam
1–2 tbs. chocolate syrup, or more to taste, optional

Place all ingredients except chocolate in a blender container and process on high until smooth. Taste and add chocolate syrup if desired. Sieve mixture before serving to remove raspberry seeds.

# FROZEN OR SLUSHY DRINKS

| | | | | |
|---|---|---|---|---|
| 85 | Raspberry Lemonade | | 95 | Banana Frost |
| 86 | Apricot Chill | | 96 | Raspberry Lemon Chill |
| 87 | Frozen Chocolate | | 97 | Minted Strawberry Freeze |
| 88 | Iced Raspberry Cream | | 98 | Mixed Fruit Fizz |
| 89 | Pineapple Sparkle | | 99 | Lime Galore |
| 90 | Blackberry Icy | | 100 | Cranberry Lime Fizz |
| 91 | Coffee Cream Frappé | | 101 | Blueberry Tang |
| 92 | Cranberry Crush | | 102 | Grape Lemonade |
| 93 | Strawberry Freeze | | 103 | Pineapple Orange Sparkle |
| 94 | Sparkling Citrus Cooler | | 104 | Blueberrry Raspberry Dream |

# RASPBERRY LEMONADE

Makes 4 cups

*To make a fast version of this drink, simply mix lemonade prepared according to the can instructions with frozen raspberries. If desired, sweeten with sugar or a little honey.*

1 cup frozen raspberries
2 cups water
½ cup chilled lemon juice
¾ cup sugar

Place all ingredients in a blender container and process until smooth. Taste and adjust sweetness. Pour through a sieve to remove seeds before serving.

# APRICOT CHILL

*Peaches or nectarines can be substituted for apricots. Keep in mind that apricots have a natural cleansing property, so don't overdo it!*

1 can (15 oz.) apricots
2¾ cups water
1½ cups sugar
1 tsp. lemon juice
1 cup cream, half-and-half, evaporated milk or milk

Drain apricots, place in a bowl, and store in the freezer until sugar syrup is ready. In a heavy saucepan, bring water and sugar to a boil; reduce heat to medium and cook for 5 minutes without stirring. Cool to room temperature.

Puree apricots until smooth, add sugar syrup mixture and lemon juice and blend for 1 minute. Pour into an ice cube tray and freeze. Pour frozen fruit cubes into a blender container, add cream and process until smooth. Taste and add more sugar or lemon juice if desired.

# FROZEN CHOCOLATE

*My grandmother used to make me "old-fashioned" cocoa for a treat. If you wish to make the fast version, use powdered cocoa mix or hot milk mixed with chocolate syrup. For an extreme chocolate version, use chocolate ice cream in place of crushed ice.*

$1/2$ cup sugar
$1/3$ cup unsweetened cocoa powder
$1/2$ cup water
$3^1/2$ cups milk
1 cup crushed ice or chocolate ice cream
sweetened whipped cream for garnish

Place sugar, cocoa powder and water in a small, heavy saucepan and stir together with a whisk. Bring to a boil and immediately stir in milk. Remove from heat, allow mixture to cool to room temperature and freeze until mixture becomes icy.

Place cocoa mixture in a blender container with ice and blend until smooth. Serve with a dollop of sweetened whipped cream.

# ICED RASPBERRY CREAM

Makes 4 cups

*This recipe uses frozen raspberries, which are available year-round. Use fresh raspberries if they are available and increase the amount of crushed ice to 1/2 cup.*

1 box (10 oz.) frozen raspberries
1 1/2 cups pineapple juice
1/4 cup crushed pineapple
1/4 cup crushed ice
2–3 tbs. coconut milk, to taste

Place all ingredients in a blender container and process on high until smooth. Taste and add more coconut milk for a creamier flavor if desired.

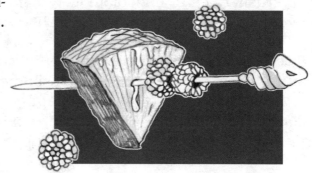

# PINEAPPLE SPARKLE

*This recipe could be increased and used as a punch. Simply place ice cream in the bottom of the punch bowl, process pineapple juice, lemon juice and sherbet in a blender and pour over ice cream along with ginger ale.*

1 cup lemon or lime sherbet
1 cup chilled pineapple juice
1 tbs. lemon juice
1 cup vanilla ice cream
1 cup ginger ale or lemon soda

Place sherbet, pineapple juice, lemon juice and ice cream in a blender container and process on high until smooth. Add ginger ale or soda and blend for 1 or 2 seconds. Serve immediately.

# BLACKBERRY ICY

*You can use loganberries, Marionberries, blueberries, raspberries or other berries in place of blackberry juice. Simply blend berries into a puree and sieve to remove seeds.*

2 cups water
½ cup sugar
1½ cups blackberry juice
2 tbs. lemon juice
½ cup cream, half-and-half, milk or coconut milk

Boil water in a heavy saucepan. Gently stir in sugar and cook on medium-high for 5 minutes. Stir in blackberry juice and lemon juice. Allow mixture to come to room temperature and pour into ice cube trays. Freeze into cubes, and then place fruit cubes in a blender container and process with cream until smooth. Serve immediately.

# COFFEE CREAM FRAPPÉ

Makes 3½ cups

*This is a simple technique, which freezes the coffee mixture and blends to a smooth cold drink with the addition of cream. For a chocolate cream frappé, hot chocolate can be substituted for coffee.*

2 cups strong coffee
½ cup sugar, or more to taste
½ cup cream, half-and-half or milk

Mix hot coffee with sugar and allow mixture to cool. Pour into ice cube trays and freeze solid. Just before serving, process frozen cubes and cream in a blender container until smooth. Taste and add more sugar or cream if desired.

# CRANBERRY CRUSH

Makes 3 cups

*Cranberries are extremely good for you and go very well with oranges. I personally like the creamier version.*

1 pkg. (12 oz.) fresh cranberries
1 1/2 cups sugar
1 cup water
2 tbs. lemon juice
1/2 cup orange juice, or more to taste
1/2 cup cream or half-and-half, optional

Place cranberries, sugar, water and lemon juice in a medium saucepan and bring to a boil. Reduce heat and cook on medium for about 12 minutes or until cranberries are soft. Pour this mixture into a blender container and puree on high until pureed. Pour into an ice cube tray and freeze. Place fruit cubes in a blender container and process along with orange juice until smooth. Taste and add more orange juice for a thinner drink if desired, or add cream for a thicker, creamier texture.

# STRAWBERRY FREEZE

Makes 2½ cups

*This drink has a potent strawberry flavor that will knock your socks off. Of course, any berry can be substituted using same berry yogurt and jam.*

1 cup frozen strawberries
1 cup frozen strawberry yogurt
2 tbs. strawberry jam
½ cup milk, soy milk, rice milk or almond milk

Place all ingredients in a blender container and process on high until smooth. Taste and add more jam for additional sweetness if desired.

# SPARKLING CITRUS COOLER

*This refreshing, cool, slushy drink is perfect for hot days. Keep a selection of these ice cubes on hand in your freezer for a quick drink when friends drop in unexpectedly. Serve with a slice of lemon or lime for garnish.*

$3/4$ cup lemonade
$3/4$ cup limeade
$3/4$ cup orange juice
2 cups lemon-lime soda

In a blender container, mix together lemonade, limeade and orange juice and process until well mixed. Pour into ice cube trays and freeze. When ready to serve, place ice cubes in blender container with soda and process until mixture is slushy.

# BANANA FROST

*This refreshing drink can be made thicker and richer by using half-and-half or cream in place of milk or yogurt. For a change, try using orange or pineapple sherbet in place of lime sherbet.*

1 1/2 cups milk, plain yogurt, half-and-half or cream
2 large bananas
1 1/2 cups lime sherbet
2 cups ginger ale

Blend together milk, bananas and sherbet on low until smooth. Add ginger ale and just barely blend. Serve in a tall glass with a slice of lime for garnish.

# RASPBERRY LEMON CHILL

Makes 3¾ cups

*This is a refreshing drink, which could be enhanced with about 1 oz. Chambord raspberry liqueur if you so desire.*

¾ cup frozen raspberries
1 cup pineapple juice, chilled
1 tbs. honey, or to taste
2 cups lemon sherbet

Place raspberries and pineapple in a blender container and process until smooth. Pour mixture into a sieve to remove seeds and then return to blender container. Add honey and lemon sherbet and process until smooth.

# MINTED STRAWBERRY FREEZE

*This easy recipe just takes minutes to fix. I tried using strawberry ice cream but it tends to overpower the taste of the mint. Use a sprig of mint or a strawberry as garnish.*

1 cup milk
1 cup vanilla ice cream or frozen yogurt
1 cup frozen strawberries
1 cup peppermint ice cream

Place milk, vanilla ice cream and strawberries in a blender container and process until smooth. Pour into glasses and float a scoop of peppermint ice cream on top.

# MIXED FRUIT FIZZ

*This is a great way to use up leftover fruit. Combine with soda and ice, taste and determine if you wish to make it creamy by adding cream or ice cream. Add a little sweetener if the fruit is not quite sweet enough.*

3 cups cubed fresh fruit (melon, plums, nectarines, grapes, papaya or other)
1 1/2 cups citrus or lemon-lime soda
1 cup crushed ice
1/4 cup cream or 1 cup ice cream or sherbet, optional
1–2 tbs. sugar or honey to taste, optional

Blend all ingredients together on high. Taste and add optional ingredients if desired.

# LIME GALORE

*This drink has a strong lime flavor and tends to be a little tart. If you like a less intense and sweeter flavor, add ice cream. A slice of lime is the perfect garnish.*

2 cups lime sherbet
1 tsp. lime juice
1 cup crushed ice
2 cups lemon-lime soda
1 cup vanilla ice cream, optional

Place sherbet, lime juice and ice in a blender container and process until smooth. Add soda and blend. Taste and make the drink creamier by adding ice cream if desired.

# CRANBERRY LIME FIZZ

*A great garnish for this drink would be a toothpick strung with cranberries and a slice of lime laid across the top of the glass.*

2 cups cranberry juice
1 cup crushed ice
1 1/2 cups lime sherbet, or more to taste
2 cups lemon-lime soda
1 cup vanilla ice cream, optional

Place juice, ice and sherbet in a blender container and process until smooth. Add soda and blend. Taste and add ice cream for a creamier flavor if desired.

# BLUEBERRY TANG

*The tang in this drink comes from the addition of an unusual ingredient, sour cream. Adding a little sugar gives this drink a sweet and sour twist. A small dollop of sour cream with a few blueberries on top would make a pretty garnish.*

2 cups blueberry juice
1½ cups crushed ice
2–3 tbs. sour cream
1 tiny pinch mace or nutmeg
1–2 tbs. sugar, or more to taste, optional

Place all ingredients except sugar in a blender container and process until smooth. Taste and add sugar if desired.

FROZEN OR SLUSHY DRINKS   101

# GRAPE LEMONADE

*A small amount of cream or vanilla ice cream can be added to this drink to create a creamier texture. Garnish this drink with a slice of lemon and a small cluster of grapes. Maple syrup gives this drink a unique flavor but sugar or honey can be substituted.*

2 cups lemonade (not the pink variety)
1 ½ cups seedless green grapes
1 tsp. lime juice
1 cup crushed ice
1–2 tbs. maple syrup, or to taste

Place all ingredients in a blender container and process on high until smooth. Taste and add more maple syrup if desired. Sieve mixture before serving.

102    FROZEN OR SLUSHY DRINKS

# PINEAPPLE ORANGE SPARKLE

*This refreshing drink could be served as a breakfast drink or after school snack. Garnish with a piece of pineapple.*

2 cups purchased pineapple-coconut juice
1 1/2 cups orange sherbet
1 cup crushed ice
1–1 1/2 cups lemon-lime soda

Place pineapple-coconut juice, sherbet and ice in a blender container and process on high until smooth. Add 1 cup of the soda and blend. Taste and add more soda if desired. For a creamier drink, increase the amount of orange sherbet.

# BLUEBERRY RASPBERRY DREAM

*This drink has a wonderful, intense flavor and would go well with muffins for breakfast.*

2 cups blueberry juice
1½ cups raspberry sherbet
1–2 tsp. lemon juice
1 cup crushed ice
½ cup cream or vanilla ice cream, optional

Place all ingredients except cream in a blender container and process on high until smooth. Taste and add cream or ice cream if desired.

# HOT DRINKS, TEAS AND CHAIS

# HOT CREAMY CAROB

*Carob is a natural alternative to hot chocolate. Brown rice syrup is readily available in health food stores and is a good replacement for sugar.*

2¹/₂ cups milk, goat's milk, soy milk or rice milk
2–3 tbs. brown rice syrup or sugar, or more to taste
2 tbs. carob powder
¹/₂–1 tsp. vanilla or chocolate extract

In a small saucepan, heat milk and rice syrup together. Pour hot mixture into a blender container. Add carob powder and extract and blend until smooth. Taste and add more rice syrup if desired.

# CRANBERRY SPICE

Makes 2½ cups

*This is a great drink for autumn and winter seasons. I like to serve it with a stick of cinnamon for garnish.*

2 cups cranberry juice
½ cup orange juice
1 tbs. honey
1 tsp. lemon juice
1 pinch cinnamon
1 pinch ground cloves
1 pinch ground cardamom

Heat cranberry juice, orange juice, honey and lemon juice in a saucepan until hot. Pour into a blender container, add spices and blend until well combined.

# COCOA CREAM

*This is a very quick version of old-fashioned chocolate. For a decadent experience, serve with a dollop of* Chocolate Whipped Cream, *page 109.*

$1/4$ cup unsweetened cocoa powder
7 oz. sweetened condensed milk
$1/4$ tsp. salt
3 cups boiling water
$1/2$ tsp. vanilla extract

Place cocoa powder, condensed milk and salt in a blender container and process for a few seconds to mix. Pour boiling water into blender container and process on high until fully incorporated. Add vanilla and process for a few seconds. Serve with marshmallows, whipped cream or *Chocolate Whipped Cream.*

108    HOT DRINKS, TEAS AND CHAIS

# CHOCOLATE WHIPPED CREAM

*Whipped cream sweetened with flavoring added is known as chantilly cream. It is excellent on coffee, chocolate, nut-flavored drinks and desserts.*

2 cups cream
$1/4$ cup unsweetened cocoa powder
$1/4$ cup granulated or confectioner's sugar
$1/2$ tsp. vanilla or almond extract

In a bowl, whip all ingredients together with a mixer and beat on high until soft peaks are formed. Refrigerate until ready to serve.

# THAI ICED TEA

*This is a very sweet, creamy tea that is a normally served with Thai food or with a variety of savory appetizers.*

2 cups boiling water
$1/8$ cup Thai tea leaves
6 oz. evaporated milk
7 oz. sweetened condensed milk, or to taste
2 cups crushed ice

In a teapot, mix together boiling water with tea leaves and allow mixture to steep for 5 minutes. Strain off tea leaves and discard. Allow mixture to come to room temperature. Blend cooled tea with evaporated milk and condensed milk until smooth. Add crushed ice and just barely blend. Serve immediately.

# CAROB MOCHA

Servings: 2

*This recipe is for people who prefer to stay caffeine-free and dairy-free. Barley malt has a flavor reminiscent of molasses. If you prefer a subtler flavor, use brown rice syrup or sugar. Tahini is a sesame seed paste which can be bought in health food stores and many of the large chain grocery stores.*

1 tbs. grain coffee (prefer Pero brand)
2 tsp. carob powder
1–2 tsp. barley malt syrup or brown rice syrup
2 tsp. tahini
2 cups boiling water

Place all ingredients in a blender container and process until smooth. Taste and add more sweetener if desired.

# TROPICAL TEA

Servings: 2

*This recipe has a tropical flavor. By changing the juices, you can create endless combinations. Serve in a tall glass with lots of ice cubes.*

2 tea bags, mango or passion fruit flavor
2 cups boiling water
1 cup chilled pineapple juice
$1/2$ cup chilled mango, passion fruit or lemon juice
honey or sugar to taste, optional

Steep tea bags in boiled water for 5 minutes. Remove bags and allow tea to come to room temperature. Pour cooled tea into a blender container. Add pineapple, mango and passion fruit juices. Blend for 15 seconds, taste and add sweetener if desired. Serve over ice cubes.

HOT DRINKS, TEAS AND CHAIS

# HOT WHITE CHOCOLATE MINT

Servings: 2

*White chocolate makes a wonderful change from typical milk chocolate cocoa. Crushed peppermint candy adds flavor and sweetness. If desired, add a peppermint stick as a stirrer.*

2 cups milk
1 oz. white chocolate
3 tbs. crushed peppermint candy
1 pinch salt
sweetened whipped cream for garnish
1 tbs. crushed peppermint candy for garnish, optional

In a saucepan, heat milk to a simmer and pour into a blender container. Add white chocolate, peppermint candy and salt. Blend until smooth and creamy. Pour into mugs and garnish with whipped cream sprinkled with crushed candy.

# CHERRY YOGURT ICED TEA

Servings: 2

*Now you can buy an assortment of delicious fruit-flavored teas that will allow you to create alternative versions of this delicious drink. Some examples would be blackberry tea with blackberry yogurt or peach tea with peach yogurt.*

3 cups boiling water
2 bags cherry tea
1 cup cherry yogurt
1 cup crushed ice
honey to taste, optional

In a heat-resistant glass container, place boiling water and tea bags. Steep for 5 to 10 minutes and then refrigerate until well chilled. Pour chilled tea mixture into a blender container and add yogurt and ice. Blend until smooth. Taste and add honey to sweeten if desired.

# HOT MINT CHOCOLATE

Servings: 2

*This is a very quick way to make hot chocolate and has an intense creamy flavor. Serve with marshmallows if desired.*

2 1/2 cups milk
1/2 cup cream
15 mint chocolate thin wafers

Place milk and cream in a saucepan and heat until mixture almost comes to a boil. Chop mint wafers into small pieces. Place all ingredients in a blender container and process until chocolate is melted and mixture is smooth.

# APRICOT TEA PUNCH

*This tea can be served either hot or cold. If you choose to serve it chilled, do not heat the apricot nectar. For a cool refresher, serve in a tall glass filled with ice cubes.*

2–3 apricot tea bags
4 cups boiling water
1 cup apricot nectar
honey or apricot preserves to sweeten, optional

Steep tea bags in boiling water for 5 to 10 minutes. Heat apricot nectar to just before boiling. Remove tea bags and pour tea into a blender container. Add apricot nectar. Blend until mixed. Taste and add sweeteners if desired.

# HOT BANANA CAROB DRINK

Makes 4 cups

*The flavors of banana, peanut butter and chocolate make a wonderful taste sensation. Carob is similar in taste to chocolate and so chocolate can be easily substituted for the carob syrup.*

3 tbs. carob powder or syrup
1 tbs. nonfat dry milk powder
2 tsp. peanut butter
$\frac{1}{2}$ banana
2 tbs. honey, or more to taste
3–4 cups hot milk, soy milk, almond milk or rice milk

Place all ingredients except hot milk in a blender container. Add 1 cup of the hot milk and process until smooth. Add 2 to 3 cups more hot milk, depending on desired thickness of drink.

# ORANGE PINEAPPLE ICED TEA

*This recipe makes a very flavorful iced tea. For an alternative, you can use other tropical frozen juice concentrates like guava, papaya or combinations of tropical fruits. Garnish with a pineapple wedge or a slice of orange.*

2 cups iced tea
2 cups water
1 can (6 oz.) frozen orange-pineapple concentrate
1 tbs. honey or sugar, or to taste, optional
fresh orange or pineapple slices for garnish

Place all ingredients except sweetener in a blender container and process until smooth. Taste and add sweetener if desired. Pour into tall glasses filled with ice cubes. Garnish with fresh fruit.

# SPICED ICED TEA

*For spiced ice coffee, coffee can be substituted for tea. For an alternative, try vanilla or coffee ice cream in place of cream.*

3 cups strong hot tea
1 three-inch piece cinnamon stick
3 cloves
4–5 tbs. sugar or honey
3/4 cup cream
ice cubes

Place tea, cinnamon stick, cloves and sugar in a bowl. Allow mixture to come to room temperature and then refrigerate until well chilled. Remove cinnamon stick and cloves and place in a blender container. Add cream and process until smooth. Serve in tall glasses filled with ice.

# CHAI TEA

Servings: 2

*The word "chai" simply means tea in India. Often Indian tea is served with equal parts tea, milk and sugar, which is a little too sweet for American tastes. This revised version reduces the sugar and adds spices for a full-flavored tea drink.*

1 cup milk
1 cup water
2 rounded tsp. black or green tea leaves
2 tsp *Spice Mix for Chai Tea*, page 121
3–4 tsp. sugar, or to taste

In a saucepan, bring milk and water to a boil. Remove pan from heat and add tea leaves and spice mix. Steep for 5 minutes. Strain into a blender container, add sugar and process until fully mixed. If desired, serve with a cinnamon stick as a stirrer.

# SPICE MIX FOR CHAI TEA

*Use this mix to spice up hot tea or iced tea mixtures. Increase or decrease any of the spices to your personal taste.*

2 tbs. cardamom seeds
2 tbs. cinnamon
4 tsp. ground ginger
4 tsp. ground cloves
1½ tsp. black pepper

Place all ingredients in a blender container and process for several minutes until mixture becomes powdery. Seal mixture in a glass jar until ready to use.

# SPICED CHAI TEA BLEND

*This mix includes the tea so you simply need to add water and milk and allow the mixture to steep. Be sure to strain tea before serving.*

2 tbs. cardamom seeds
1 tbs. whole cloves
¾–1 tbs. black peppercorns
1 stick cinnamon (3–4 inch)

pinch of ginger powder (or more to taste)
1 cup loose black or green tea leaves

Place all ingredients except tea leaves in a blender container and process until ingredients are powdered. Stir in tea leaves. Store in a sealed glass container until ready to serve.

## TO SERVE
Servings: 2

¾ cup milk
¾ cup water

2 rounded tsp. spiced chai tea blend
2–3 tsp. sugar or honey, or to taste

In a saucepan, bring milk and water to a boil. Remove from heat, add tea blend and steep for 5 minutes. Strain tea before serving and add desired amount of sugar.

# QUICK CHAI TEA

*This recipe simply adds all the ingredients together (without a mix) to make a quick cup of sweet, spiced tea. Use fresh cardamom pods for the best flavor.*

8 cardamom pods
1 1/2 cups water
2-inch piece cinnamon stick
8 whole cloves
1 tbs. black tea leaves
3/4–1 cup milk
1–2 tsp. sugar or honey, or to taste

Slightly crush cardamom pods to allow the seeds to be exposed. Place pods in a saucepan and add water, cinnamon stick and cloves. Bring to a boil, cover and reduce heat. Simmer for 10 minutes. Remove pan from heat, add tea leaves and steep for 5 minutes. Strain into a blender container, add milk and sugar and blend to mix. Taste and add more sweetener if desired.

# SUPER CREAMY DRINKS AND FLOATS

125    Pineapple Cream Shake
126    Praline Creamsicle
127    Strawberry Dream
128    Banana Colada Cream
129    Apricot Ambrosia
130    Blender Eggnog
131    Blueberry Cream
132    Boysenberry Apple Cream
133    Coconut-Pineapple Cream
134    Fruited Cranberry Shake
135    Orange Creamsicle
136    Coffee Banana Shake
137    Ginger Peach Shake
138    Deadly Chocolate Cream
139    Creamy Orange Fizz
140    Root Beer Melon Cream
141    Cantaloupe Maple Cream
142    Apple Maple Cream

# PINEAPPLE CREAM SHAKE

Makes 6 cups

*If you choose to use pineapple chunks or fresh pineapple, be sure to strain the mixture before drinking. Pineapple can tend to have a stringy texture even when you blend for several minutes. You may need to make this in two batches if your blender capacity is limited.*

2 cups canned crushed pineapple
2 cups vanilla ice cream or pineapple sherbet
2 cups milk or pineapple juice
4 tsp. lemon juice or lime juice
1 tbs. sugar or honey, optional

In a blender container, blend all ingredients on high until smooth. Taste and add more sweetener if desired.

SUPER CREAMY DRINKS AND FLOATS    125

# PRALINE CREAMSICLE

*Sometimes caramel sauce does not blend well, so be sure to warm the sauce before blending. If you wish, garnish with a dollop of whipped cream that has been sweetened with brown sugar and sprinkled with chopped toasted pecans.*

2 cups milk
1 1/2 cups praline ice cream
1/3 cup caramel sauce, warmed
2 tbs. chocolate syrup

Place all ingredients in a blender container and process on high until well combined. For a thicker shake, increase amount of ice cream.

# STRAWBERRY DREAM

*Fresh strawberries are best for this recipe, but if you use frozen strawberries, reduce the crushed ice to 1 cup. This drink is creamy enough without ice cream, so try a sip before adding the cream and determine if you want the added richness.*

2 cups fresh strawberries
1/4 cup fresh lemon juice
1 1/2 cups crushed ice
1 cup sweetened condensed milk
1 cup strawberry ice cream, optional
1/2–1 cup milk to thin mixture, optional

Place strawberries, lemon juice, crushed ice and condensed milk in a blender container and process on high until smooth. Taste and add ice cream if desired. For a thinner drink, add milk.

# BANANA COLADA CREAM

*This is similar to a piña colada but bananas are used instead of orange juice. The addition of lemon juice helps to sharpen the taste of the fruit.*

2 bananas, cut up
1 cup cold pineapple juice
1 cup crushed ice
3/4 cup sweetened condensed milk
1/4 cup fresh lemon juice
2 tbs. coconut milk
1 cup banana or vanilla ice cream or yogurt, optional

Blend bananas, pineapple juice, ice, condensed milk, lemon juice and coconut milk together until smooth. Taste and add ice cream if desired.

# APRICOT AMBROSIA

*This recipe would also work with pureed peaches or nectarines in place of the apricot nectar. Make sure the juice is well chilled.*

1 can (16 oz.) apricot nectar
1 can (8 oz.) club soda
1/3 cup sweetened condensed milk
1 cup vanilla ice cream or frozen yogurt
1 tbs. honey, optional

Place all ingredients in a blender container and process until smooth. Taste and add honey for sweetness if desired.

# BLENDER EGGNOG

Makes 3½ cups

*It is important to cook eggs nowadays because of the salmonella scare. This recipe cooks a base mixture, which can be refrigerated until ready to serve. The chilled mixture is poured into a blender container and thinned with milk to desired thickness. Then, if desired, add alcohol to taste.*

2 cups half-and-half
½ cup cream
⅔ cup sugar
4 egg yolks
1½ tsp. pure vanilla extract

¼ tsp. nutmeg, or to taste
½ cup milk, or more to taste
dark rum, bourbon or brandy to taste, optional

In a blender container, place half-and-half, cream, sugar and egg yolks and process until mixture turns pale yellow. Pour into a heavy saucepan and cook on medium, stirring constantly, until mixture thickens and leaves a path on back of spoon when a finger is drawn across. Stir in vanilla and nutmeg and refrigerate until ready to serve. To serve, pour chilled mixture into blender along with milk. Add alcohol if desired. Blend until smooth. Taste and add more nutmeg if desired.

# BLUEBERRY CREAM

*This recipe uses a slightly different technique of whipping the cream and folding in the remaining ingredients, so you end up with a very fluffy, creamy drink. The ice cream is generally served as a garnish on top of the drink, but it can be blended in with the blueberries if you wish.*

1½ cups heavy cream
1 cup frozen blueberries
2 cups milk
2 tbs. honey or sugar
1 cup vanilla ice cream or frozen yogurt

Place cream in a bowl and beat until whipped cream holds soft peaks. Set aside. In a blender container, blend together blueberries, milk and honey. Pour blueberry mixture over whipped cream and fold together. Serve in a tall glass with a scoop of ice cream.

# BOYSENBERRY APPLE CREAM

Makes 4½ cups

*If boysenberries are not available for this recipe you can use loganberries, Marionberries or raspberries. Also, try using alternative flavors of ice cream, frozen yogurt, sorbet or sherbet.*

1 cup fresh or frozen boysenberries or boysenberry juice
1 cup apple juice
2½ cups vanilla or berry ice cream
1 pinch cinnamon or nutmeg
1–2 tbs. honey or boysenberry jam, optional

Place all ingredients in a blender container and process until smooth. If using whole berries, sieve the mixture to remove seeds before serving. Taste and add sweetener if desired. Garnish with whipped cream and a few berries.

# COCONUT PINEAPPLE CREAM

Makes 2½ cups

*This recipe is somewhat reminiscent of a piña colada. For a variation, try substituting pineapple sherbet for ice cream. If you prefer not to have small bits of pineapple in your drink, sieve before serving.*

½ cup canned crushed pineapple
1 cup vanilla frozen yogurt or ice cream
1 cup milk or pineapple juice
2 tbs. coconut cream
½ tsp. pure vanilla extract
1 pinch nutmeg, optional
1 tbs. sugar or honey, or to taste, optional

Place pineapple in a blender container and process until mushy. Add yogurt, milk, coconut cream, vanilla and nutmeg if desired. Process until smooth and creamy. Taste and add sweetener if desired.

# FRUITED CRANBERRY SHAKE

Makes 5½ cups

*For this drink, it is important to chill the juices before mixing. Orange sherbet can be substituted for pineapple sherbet. Increase the ice cream if you wish a thicker and creamier shake.*

1 cup cranberry juice
1 cup pineapple juice
½ cup apricot nectar
2 cups vanilla ice cream or frozen yogurt
1 cup pineapple sherbet or sorbet.

Place all ingredients in a blender container and process until smooth.

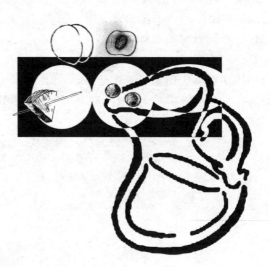

# ORANGE CREAMSICLE

Makes 5 cups

*Sometimes for a dessert, I will mix vanilla ice cream and orange sherbet togeth-er. This drink was created with that dessert in mind. This is a favorite with children.*

1 can (6 oz.) frozen orange juice concentrate
1 cup vanilla ice cream or frozen yogurt
1 cup orange sherbet
$1/4$–$1/2$ cup cream or milk
2 cups ginger ale

Place all ingredients except ginger ale in a blender container and process until smooth. Just before serving, whirl in ginger ale. Do not over-process, as this will remove carbonation. Taste and add more milk to thin if desired.

# COFFEE BANANA SHAKE

*This drink is a great breakfast pick-me-up! Top with whipped cream for garnish and a slice of banana or a chocolate-covered coffee bean.*

2 cups cold coffee
2 cups vanilla ice cream or frozen yogurt
2 fresh or frozen bananas, cut into pieces
1 tsp. pure banana or vanilla extract
3–4 tbs. honey or sweetener of choice

Place all ingredients in a blender container and process until smooth. Taste and add more sweetener if desired.

# GINGER PEACH SHAKE

*Candied ginger can be substituted for ginger powder here if you wish a more intense flavor. Simply blend 1 or 2 pieces of candied ginger until finely chopped before adding the other ingredients. Garnish with whipped cream and a sprinkle of cinnamon.*

1 cup canned or fresh peaches, sliced
1 cup milk or half-and-half
2 cups peach or vanilla ice cream
2 tbs. brown sugar
1/4 tsp. ginger powder
1 pinch cinnamon

Place all ingredients in a blender container and process until smooth.

# DEADLY CHOCOLATE CREAM

*Chocolate upon chocolate — what more could you want! This recipe uses dark chocolate but milk chocolate ice cream or fudge sauces can be substituted to create a less "intense" flavor. Garnish with* Chocolate Whipped Cream *and either chocolate chips, grated chocolate, chocolate covered nuts or crushed candy bars.*

2 cups chocolate milk
2 cup dark chocolate ice cream
2 tbs. chocolate syrup
few drops of vanilla
1 pinch cinnamon, optional
*Chocolate Whipped Cream,* page 109, for garnish

Place all ingredients except garnish in a blender container and process until smooth. Garnish with *Chocolate Whipped Cream* and any desired extras.

# CREAMY ORANGE FIZZ

Makes: 5-6 cups

*This recipe makes an easy punch that is great for a party. Garnish with a slice of orange on the side of a chilled glass or, for larger quantities, add several slices of orange and a few sprigs of mint or a few maraschino cherries.*

2 cups orange juice
2 cups lemon-lime soda
1–2 cups vanilla ice cream, to taste

Place all ingredients in a blender container and process on high until smooth. Adjust ice cream to taste.

# ROOT BEER MELON CREAM

Makes: 4½ cups

*Whoever thought that watermelon and root beer would taste so good? Be sure to chill the watermelon and root beer before blending. Garnish with a slice of watermelon.*

2 cups diced seedless watermelon
1½ cups root beer
1 cup vanilla ice cream
½ cup crushed ice

Place all ingredients in a blender container and process on high until smooth. Serve immediately.

# CANTALOUPE MAPLE CREAM

*Fresh mixed fruit can be substituted for cantaloupe if desired. I have even used left-over fruit salad as an alternative. Garnish with a slice of cantaloupe.*

3 cups diced cantaloupe
$1/2$–1 cup cream, vanilla ice cream or vanilla yogurt
1 tbs. fresh lemon juice
1 cup lemon-lime soda
1–2 tbs. maple syrup, or more to taste
$1/2$ cup crushed ice

Peel, seed and finely dice cantaloupe. Place all ingredients in a blender container and process on high until smooth. You may need to increase maple syrup depending on the sweetness of the cantaloupe.

# APPLE MAPLE CREAM

Makes: 3 cups

*I prefer to use purchased fresh-squeezed apple juice or unfiltered bottled apple juice in this recipe. Garnish with a piece of apple that has been rubbed with lemon juice to keep apple from turning brown.*

2 cups chilled apple juice
1 cup vanilla ice cream or frozen yogurt
1 tbs. maple syrup, or to taste
1 pinch cinnamon
1 tiny pinch nutmeg

Place all ingredients in a blender container and process on high until smooth. Taste and add more syrup or spices if desired.

# INDEX

143

## Notes and Favorite Blender Drink Recipes

# Notes and Favorite Blender Drink Recipes

# Notes and Favorite Blender Drink Recipes

# Notes and Favorite Blender Drink Recipes

# Notes and Favorite Blender Drink Recipes

# Notes and Favorite Blender Drink Recipes

## Notes and Favorite Blender Drink Recipes

## Notes and Favorite Blender Drink Recipes

# Serve Creative, Easy, Nutritious Meals with **nitty gritty**® Cookbooks

1 or 2, Cooking for
100 Dynamite Desserts
9 x 13 Pan Cookbook
Asian Cooking
Bagels, Best
Barbecue Cookbook
Beer and Good Food
Big Book Kitchen Appliance
Big Book Snack, Appetizer
Blender Drinks
Bread Baking
New Bread Machine Book
Bread Machine III
Bread Machine V
Bread Machine VI
Bread Machine, Entrees
Burger Bible
Cappuccino/Espresso
Casseroles
Chicken, Unbeatable
Chile Peppers
Cooking in Clay

Coffee and Tea
Convection Oven
Cook-Ahead Cookbook
Crockery Pot, Extra-Special
Deep Fryer
Dessert Fondues
Edible Gifts
Edible Pockets
Fabulous Fiber Cookery
Fondue and Hot Dips
Fondue, New International
Freezer, 'Fridge, Pantry
Garlic Cookbook
Grains, Cooking with
Healthy Cooking on Run
Ice Cream Maker
Irish Pub Cooking
Italian, Quick and Easy
Juicer Book II
Kids, Cooking with Your
Kids, Healthy Snacks for
Loaf Pan, Recipes for

Low-Carb
No Salt No Sugar No Fat
Party Foods/Appetizers
Pasta Machine Cookbook
Pasta, Quick and Easy
Pinch of Time
Pizza, Best
Porcelain, Cooking in
Pressure Cooker
Rice Cooker
Salmon Cookbook
Sandwich Maker
Simple Substitutions
Slow Cooking
Slow Cooker, Vegetarian
Soups and Stews
Soy & Tofu Recipes
Tapas Fantásticas
Toaster Oven Cookbook
Waffles & Pizzelles
Wedding Catering book
Wraps and Roll-Ups